FIRE IN THE RED LAND

Two-Act Play:
The Life of
Saint Mary of the Cross MacKillop

Margaret Therese Cusack rsj

2017

Adelaide

First Edition: Copyright 1979

Revised edition: Copyright 1994

Third revised edition 2017

FIRE IN THE RED LAND (The Life of Saint Mary MacKillop)

Author: Margaret Therese Cusack rsj

1. Written and Produced:

1979: Bankstown Theatre Hall, Sydney NSW and the Auditorium, Catholic Teachers' College, North Sydney NSW
Cast: Actors from Revesby Parish, Rockdale and Doonside, suburbs of Sydney
Producer: Sr Margaret Therese Cusack rsj
Director: Fr JW O'Neill

2. Revised and assessed version: through the National Playwright Centre NSW.

1995: Produced for three nights at Penola, South Australia
Cast: Penola Players
Producer/Director: Mr Brian Larkin

First Edition: 1979

Second Edition: 1994

Third Edition: 2017

Published by:

An imprint of the ATF Press Publishing
Group owned by ATF (Australia) Ltd.
PO Box 504
Hindmarsh, SA 5007
ABN 90 116 359 963
www.atfpress.com
Making a lasting impact

Foreword

Fire in the Red Land is a two Act play about an Australian named Mary MacKillop. The daughter of Scottish migrants, she was born in Fitzroy, Melbourne in 1842 and she was declared the first Australian Saint by the Catholic Church in 2010. This dramatic presentation by playwright Margaret Therese Cusack rsj offers an overview of some of the happenings in Mary MacKillop's life story and gives an insight into the religious beliefs and values that motivated her endeavours.

In her introduction, Margaret Therese Cusack mentions that the genesis of this theatre production lay in her appointment as a promoter of the knowledge of Mary MacKillop's life story. During the late nineteenth century, she and Catholic priest, Julian Tenison Woods founded the Sisters of St Joseph of the Sacred Heart and in 1977, the Pope's representative in Australia informed the leadership of this Catholic Institute of Religious that it was their task to make Mary MacKillop known to the Australian public.

The aim of the promotion was to offer this Australian woman to all Australians, irrespective of religious affiliation. With this in mind, the creator of the play has been keen to present a script that is historically correct and to this end has used words and phrases taken from Mary MacKillop's writings. Mary understood the issues of her time, the difficulties faced by the labouring class when trying to find work, the lack of formal education available to children in isolated settlements, and the growing emphasis on acquiring wealth because of the status in society that it offered as well as a subtle secularity that tended to weaken religious belief. Her vision of a united community that respected the dignity of each individual and responded to the needs of the poorest motivated her actions. She strongly believed that God had a personal love for each individual and endeavoured to respond to whatever life presented with courage and trust.

Over the years *Fire in the Red Land* has been revised and refined so that this play can be presented as a professional script. As such it is offered to adult theatre groups and senior school groups. Even though children are members of the cast, its content, except for a few scenes, seems unsuitable for primary school presentation.

May those who take part in performance of this play and those who view it catch some of the fire that motivated St Mary of the Cross MacKillop.

Margaret M. McKenna rsj

"FIRE IN THE RED LAND" THEME

Chorus: *Fr JW O'Neill;*
Verses: *Margaret Therese Cusack rsj*

Chorus:
Fire in the Red Land,
Kindled by Spirit's Power
Caught by a loving hand
Fanned to consuming desire
Children's praise swells up to you.
Hail to our mother in God.

1. *She was born in the Red Land,*
Nurtured at God's Hand,
Mary had a vision of the children's need.
There was poverty and hardship, sickness and suffering,
Loneliness that many people wouldn't heed.

2. *A Priest of God in the days of the gold rush*
Shared Mary's dream of Australia in unity.
His missionary heart on fire with Christ-love
Led him to believe in the power of community.

3. *Before Federation, Mary shared that vision*
God's burning love she longed that all would see
A new congregation fanned the inspiration
Given by the spirit to set God's people free.

INTRODUCTION

Genesis of the Play
In 1978, I was co-opted by the Provincial of the Sisters of St Joseph in the southern region of Sydney to promote the cause for the beatification of Mary MacKillop. One way of doing this was through the media. A dramatic production came to mind.

A priest in the Parish of Panania in the Archdiocese of Sydney, Fr JW O'Neill had just written and produced a play with his drama group. He began to write the play: ***"Fire in the Red Land"*** and gave it the title, but preferred that I write it, as he considered I had more background knowledge of Mary MacKillop's life. Fr O'Neill also wrote the chorus for its theme song.

I wrote it in Term One, 1979. Fr O'Neill agreed to direct it with a cast comprising actors from several dramatic and musical societies, including the Rocks Players and Rockdale Musical Society. Many parishioners and children from Revesby Parish in the Archdiocese of Sydney volunteered their services. After each scene I submitted the text to Srs Teresita Cormack rsj, Evelyn Pickering rsj and Anne-Marie Power rsj for the checking of historical accuracy. The Director proofread the script for dramatic effectiveness.

The play was performed in 1979 at Bankstown Theatre Hall (two nights) and at Mount Street, North Sydney NSW (one night later that year). The cast had prepared for it during Term Two of that year. Following the production, many of the participants expressed a deep appreciation and love of Mary MacKillop

Revised Script (completed 1994)
After having sent this script to the Australian National Playwrights Centre (ANPC) for critical assessment, I have revised and refined it considerably. Its length was severely reduced, the plot was tightened and the doubling of characters for any future productions was recommended. The Historical Society in Penola, South Australia, took it up and had it produced and directed by Mr Brian Larkin with a cast of local players. There were three successful amateur performances in January 1995, in the week prior to the Beatification of Blessed Mary MacKillop.

I am grateful to the critics at the Playwrights Centre for their helpful advice. Even so, I have left a fairly large cast in the play, including the children, as I feel that, with further reductions, I would lose the aspect of the love of children and rapport with them that was a highlight of Mary MacKillop's life. I hope that audiences will catch the spirit which characterised our first Australian to be canonised, and that many amateur groups and secondary schools may see this play as a worthwhile way to explore such a magnificent life.

Assistance with Publication
Sincere thanks are due to the many people who have helped bring this work to publication. They include Maryellen Thomas rsj from the Congregational Leadership Team; proof-readers Marie Foale rsj and Margaret McKenna rsj; those who did the necessary formatting and artistic work, Jen Walker, Nora Carrigan and Sandy Leaitua; and archivists Roslyn Kennedy, North Sydney, NSW and Claire Larkin, Penola, SA for their supply of photographs. I also offer sincere gratitude to the producers, directors, actors, stage managers, lighting technicians, musicians and costumiers who have worked with the play over the years. These people have greatly enhanced the production and brought to life the passion of St Mary of the Cross MacKillop for education and her love for the poor.

FIRE IN THE RED LAND

I have chosen segments of Mary's life which highlight Mary's respect for people and love for the poor. Mary ages from twenty-three years to sixty-seven years.

SYNOPSIS

ACT 1

The Spark is Lit

SCENE 1: FITZROY COTTAGE, PORTLAND, VIC.
The scene is Fitzroy Cottage where Mary is living with two boarders while the rest of the family is at Bayview House with four boarders.[1]

SCENE 2: WINELLA COTTAGE, PENOLA SA (1866)
In this scene, we see the directness, simplicity and single-mindedness of Mary, who was ready to forge ahead, despite opposition, even from the members of her own family. [2]

SCENE 3: THE HOME OF THE BOURKE FAMILY, PENOLA SA
Mary is shown as a warm, compassionate woman whose genuine love for God's people showed itself in her passion for the education of the poor and kindness to the less fortunate. The people with whom she came in contact felt the fire of God's love and peace beyond understanding, coming from her deep spirit of prayer and union with Jesus. Mary's love for the unwanted was a particular quality evident in her life and work.[3]

Fire of Christ's Love

SCENE 4: PELHAM COTTAGE, ADELAIDE SA
The Profession of Mary of the Cross MacKillop
Father Woods presided at this simple ceremony with the permission of Bishop Sheil and Father Smyth, Parish Priest of Adelaide, South Australia. He based it on the one used in the Passionist Order, of which he had been a member.[4]

SCENE 5: FRANKLIN STREET, ADELAIDE, SA: THE EXCOMMUNICATION OF MARY OF THE CROSS

a) Private encounter with Fr Horan
b) The Excommunication
c) Mary's Response

The situation highlights the Christlike attitude of Mary, who does not resent the action of others, but loves them and prays for them.[5]

1. Osmund Thorpe, *Mary MacKillop: The Life of Mother Mary of the Cross* (London Burns & Oates, 1957), 26.
2. Thorpe, *Mary MacKillop,* 28.
3. Dialogue fictional, but based on the tradition of Mary's kindness to the less fortunate.
4. Profession script adapted from Archival record of ceremony, 1875.
5. Sisters of St Joseph, eds, *Resource Material from the Archives of the Sisters of St Joseph of the Sacred Heart, No. 4* (Booklet, Sisters of St Joseph, North Sydney, August 1980), 54–61

ACT 2

SCENE 1: KENSINGTON CONVENT IN ADELAIDE SA (1875)

In this scene Mary has just arrived at Kensington after her overseas journey. She and the fifteen Irish postulants who had come with her had landed in Melbourne on the previous Christmas Day after a long sea journey around the Cape of Good Hope and had reached Adelaide early in the New Year.
Mary reminisces with her old friends, Srs Monica Phillips rsj and Calasanctius Howley rsj (novice mistress and superior respectively), about all that had happened.[6]

SCENE 2: HOTEL SCENE, WILMINGTON, EN ROUTE TO PORT AUGUSTA SA (1878)

In 1878, Mother Mary of the Cross travels from Adelaide in haste to the bedside of two young Sisters who have been badly burned from the explosion of a lamp in the church. Mother Mary is delayed on her journey when the coach stops at Wilmington, still some distance from Port Augusta, and calls into a hotel to ask for help to finish the journey. *Mary does arrive in time to comfort Sister Laurentia Honner rsj before her death at the age of nineteen and then stays on for a whole week to comfort her companion, Sister Immaculata Punyer rsj.* Mary's genuine love for her Sisters was shown by action in this scene.[7]

SCENE 3: MOUNT STREET CONVENT, NORTH SYDNEY NSW

Mary, as an older, sick woman, renews her friendship with an older Jane Bourke.[8]

Finale: Mount Street Convent, North Sydney NSW

This scene depicts the visit of the boys from Kincumber Orphanage.[9]
Reference to Philip is to a true story of Mary's visit to a dying fifteen-year-old boy at Kincumber. He is buried in the Kincumber cemetery.

---

6. Thorpe, *Mary MacKillop,* 175.
7. Cathy Oliver ed, *Memories of Mary by those who knew her, Sisters of St Joseph, 1925–1926* (Mulgrave, Vic. JohnGarratt Publishers, 2010), 21 & 27.
8. Dialogue fictional, based on archival evidence of Mary's faithfulness to people in her life.
9. Dialogue fictional, based on archival reports of Kincumber boys' visits to Mary at North Sydney.

SETTING
A black curtain is used as a backdrop for each scene, and lighting effects are used e.g. spotlight in some scenes. The settings are as follows:

ACT 1

SCENE 1: FITZROY COTTAGE, PORTLAND VIC.
Room in the house

SCENE 2: WINELLA COTTAGE, PENOLA SA (1866)
Kitchen, kitchen table

SCENE 3: THE HOME OF THE BOURKE FAMILY, PENOLA SA
Bed, kitchen/pot-belly stove, chairs

SCENE 4: PROFESSION SCENE: PELHAM COTTAGE, GROTE STREET, ADELAIDE SA
Spotlight on Cross against black curtain; cushion as kneeler for Mary

SCENE 5: FRANKLIN STREET CONVENT, ADELAIDE SA

(a) Private encounter before excommunication: table, two chairs
(b) The event: kneeler, pews, altar

ACT 2

SCENE 1: KENSINGTON CONVENT, ADELAIDE SA
Three chairs; two or three mattresses on floor. Sr Mary is now known as Mother Mary.

SCENE 2: HOTEL BAR AND CHAIR (ILLUSION OF OTHER IN THE BAR COULD BE DONE BY SIMPLE PROP AND USE OF SPOTLIGHT)

SCENE 3: MOUNT STREET CONVENT, NORTH SYDNEY NSW

(a) Jane enters: Desk, statue of St Joseph, wheelchair
An old typewriter (Archives, Mount Street, North Sydney has the original)
(b) Kincumber boys enter: same

FIRE IN THE RED LAND

(LIGHT ON ORCHESTRA)

"FIRE IN THE RED LAND" THEME: PIANO OVERTURE [OR ORGAN]

THE SPARK IS LIT

ACT 1

SCENE 1: FITZROY COTTAGE (SEPTEMBER 1865–SATURDAY)

(VOICE OVER: MARY MACKILLOP)
The story I am about to share with you has a stormy prelude. In the middle of September 1865, when I was twenty-three years of age, there was a family crisis and some final decisions had to be made. Father Woods arrived in Portland from Penola in South Australia, where I had met and talked with him some four years earlier.

He was a provident instrument in opening up the way of fulfilment of a heavenly promise. This was the beginning of the Penola venture.

(MARY, AGED TWENTY-THREE, LIVES IN FITZROY COTTAGE, PORTLAND AND HAS TWO BOARDERS LIVING WITH HER: LIZZIE O'REILLY AND KATE NOLAN. MARY IS SWEEPING THE FLOOR... A KNOCK AT THE DOOR INTERRUPTS HER)

MARY: (GOES TO THE DOOR) Why, Father Woods! This is indeed a pleasant surprise!

FR WOODS: Mary, I've just been down at Bay View House, after riding in from Penola. I was talking to the rest of the family, and met four boarders staying with them. Annie told me that you had two girls staying with you here... so the family is more or less together for the moment?

MARY: Yes, but not for long, I fear; it's a long story, Father. I did try to fill you in on some of the detail in my letters, but at the moment, we seem to have reached another crisis. We'll have to sell up the Bay View Cottage, it seems. But, anyhow, how are you? You look weary after your journey.

FR WOODS: Not so much tired as concerned at the moment, Mary. You see, I'm looking for a teacher who would be willing to take over the school in Penola. Miss Mattie Johnson resigned because she was getting married, and her sister has just given notice for the same reason. What I'm getting around to asking, Mary, is: Would you help me out? I've asked you this before, but the situation is even more urgent.

MARY: It's not that I don't want to go to Penola, Father, but what is worrying me at the moment is Mamma, Papa and the family. I've wanted so much for us to be together, and, I'm afraid I've lost patience with Papa many times. Because of his mismanagement, we are in more debt. He spent the money that grandfather had given us for the piano, (thinking it was his!), and now we can't afford to keep the Bay View House. We cannot even find another boarder!

FR WOODS: It does look, sad as it may seem, as if your family will have to break up in order to survive, Mary. I know that this is a painful Cross the Lord is giving you, though I have no doubt you will come closer to Him through it.

MARY: (THOUGHTFULLY) It is indeed something I'll have to face. Going to Penola is my one desire, but there seem to be far too many obstacles. When were you thinking I might go?

FR WOODS: I was hoping that it would be next year.

MARY: Next year!

FR WOODS: Maybe Annie could help out till the end of the year to give you a chance to get things settled here. What about it, Mary? And what's this about the Bay View House?

MARY: Well, as you can see, Father, Mamma will find it impossible to cope with the rearing of the two boys, Donald and Peter, without my help. Maggie is still very ill and needs constant care. John's twenty, and still out of a job. It won't work.

FR WOODS: I'm sure we can work something out. Anyway, Mary, you don't need to worry about John. I have an idea that I can get him some work in Penola. Lexie could go and join Annie. It certainly looks as if your father will have to leave Portland, at least temporarily, if your mother is to cope financially. Later on, I might be able to get the boys into Sevenhill, with the Jesuits.

MARY: That would be wonderful for them if you could, thanks, Father, but that's in the future. For now, though I hate to think of it, I might be able to persuade Papa to go to Uncle Peter's place at Hamilton... and could Uncle Peter look after Maggie at Lara until she is well enough to join us? Oh, I find it heartbreaking that we should be separated like this! It was so good when we were at the Bay View House together.

FR WOODS: Mary, I have the greatest confidence in St Joseph that all will work out for the best in the end. He will take our needs to his Son... I'll have to be off now... (PICKS UP HIS COAT, ETC) I assure you that you and your family are in my daily prayer and especially the Mass. I'm convinced that the Lord has a special work for you to do, that only you can do for him, Mary, and I hope you won't put him off for too long. I will pray for you, and *do sit more closely under the shadow of the Cross*. God be with you, Mary!

MARY: (HANDING HIM HIS BAG) And you too, Father. Thank you for calling.
I will give all you have said thought and prayer, Father, and let you know as soon as I can.

(Tape of Verse 2)

A Priest of God in the days of the gold rush
Shared Mary's dream of Australia in unity
His missionary heart on fire with Christ-love
Led him to believe in the power of community.

(FATHER WOODS EXIT)

MARY: (KNEELS, PRAYS ALOUD) Father in Heaven, if you want me for this special service to you, show me the way. Help me to have the courage to give up everything, no matter how hard it is, so that I can do what you want of me. The way is so uncertain... yet I do believe that you have sent Fr Woods to show me the way I must follow. He told me that I was putting you off... please give me light and strength to see where I must go from here, and to go where you are calling me. The finances are a big worry to me. I can't see any answers. *Only what you will, my God. Use me as you will.*

(VOICE OF JOHN, OFF-STAGE)
Are you there, Mary? (MARY RISES)

MARY: Why, John, it's good to see you! I've just had a visit from Father Woods.
(JOHN COMES IN AND SITS DOWN)
Did he mention anything to you about going to Penola?

JOHN: Yes, but he said he would have to discuss the matter with you before he finalised anything. What do <u>you</u> think of it all, Mary?

MARY: Well, John, you remember my first experiences in Penola with Aunt Margaret Cameron on the governess job. Since then, I've still the urge to go and do something over there about the education of the Penola children. They haven't any way of being educated, particularly in their faith. The poverty's deplorable, and the ignorance... Father Woods seems to have the whole region on his own, where the faith is concerned, from Mount Gambier to the River Murray.

JOHN: I thought that you'd given up the idea of going over there long ago.
(MARY LOOKS INTENTLY AT JOHN)

MARY: John, you know I can't dismiss the idea... even though we're in so much debt. Papa taught us so much about our ordinary education and our faith, and I feel called to spread the Good News in a special way. Father Woods assures me that we will be able to handle the debts somehow. Did he ask you to come to Penola too?

JOHN: Yes, he did, Mary. He's convinced me that it would be worthwhile for you to get things started over there. Father Woods has high hopes of getting me a job there, too, to help pay off some of our debts.

MARY: That would be good. I'll have to talk to Annie about the teaching position from now until the end of the year.

JOHN: I think she's ready to take the job, if necessary, but if I know Annie, she's not willing to take over anything of this nature permanently.

MARY: Annie may not, but I'm still thinking seriously of becoming a Sister, though the kind of life I think we'll need to lead in Penola... visiting the people and travelling to different homesteads and settlements would hardly fit in with traditional convent life such as we know in Victoria and New South Wales.

JOHN: Maybe you'll have to start something new?

MARY: (PAUSES IN WONDER) Who knows where this venture will finally lead, John?

JOHN: What about Papa?

MARY: I've discussed the matter with Father Woods, and I think we might be able to get him to go to Hamilton, and Maggie to Uncle Peter in Lara.

JOHN: I hope it all works out for the best, Well, Mary, it looks as if I'd better be getting back now. Maggie's not the best.

MARY: Tell Mamma that I'll be down shortly to talk over the whole matter. Mamma will suffer much over this. She doesn't want me to go. We must pray that it is His will, not ours.

JOHN: Yes, Mary, but will you ever be able to go?

(AUDIO OF VERSE 1 OF "FIRE IN THE RED LAND" THEME)

She was born in the Red Land, nurtured at God's Hand,
Mary had a vision of the children's need.
There was poverty and hardship, sickness and suffering,
Loneliness that many people wouldn't heed.

ACT 1

SCENE 2: WINELLA COTTAGE (PENOLA, EARLY NOVEMBER 1866)

(AT THIS TIME, MARY WEARS A LONG BLACK DRESS AND A LEATHER BELT. THE OTHER GIRLS WEAR THE ORDINARY LONG DRESS OF THE DAY. MARY AND ANNIE ARE IN THE KITCHEN, SITTING AT THE TABLE DOING THE VEGETABLES FOR DINNER. MARY IS 24, ANNIE IS 18, AND MAGGIE IS 23)

(VOICE OVER: MARY MACKILLOP)
The family in crisis put the seal on the event of my choice to go to Penola in 1866, to take charge of 55 poor children, hoping that somehow the debts could be paid off from there, as Father Woods assured me. Annie had gone the previous year, and my sister Lexie and I travelled in 1866 to join her at Winella Cottage. Maggie joined us later that year. I began to wear subdued black—in those days a sign of the choice I had made of the Religious Life.

ANNIE: Well, Mary, just from hearing what the parents are saying, people are getting the message that you are beginning a new order of Sisters.

MARY: Yes, Annie, I'm glad about that, really, because it will spread elsewhere, and there may be other girls who would want to join; but our relations don't seem too happy about this venture, with the exception of Uncle Donald. All the others have found excuses for not helping out.

ANNIE: Mary, you must admit that you are going about things differently from the accepted idea of Sisters.

MARY: Yes, I realise that... It's certainly not Religious Life as it is traditionally known.

ANNIE: It's just unheard of for Sisters to be seen in the streets and lanes of the town. Why can't you choose something more acceptable?

MARY: As Father Woods explained to me earlier, the monastic customs are just unsuitable for our kind of work among the settlers. The need for visitation is so urgent. The Sisters of St Joseph from Auvergne in France are living like we are, he said, more like the style of St Francis of Assisi.

ANNIE: That takes me back to the money side of things, Mary. What guarantee is there of being able to keep going as a voluntary service in this part of the country? Who's going to put money behind such a gamble? We've never had enough to make ends meet here. It's just not practical.

MARY: Well, I'm concerned about the debts, Annie. The boarders at Fitzroy Cottage in Portland are the only source of income for Mamma, and we're up against a bill of one hundred pounds still, even though Father Woods did promise he would see to the debt.

ANNIE: One hundred pounds is a lot of money, Mary, I don't know. Things are not going to get any easier while neither Maggie, Lexie, nor I are receiving any income. John's finding it very difficult to keep himself in New Zealand, according to this letter.
(PICKS UP THE LETTER FROM THE TABLE)

MARY: I wish he had stayed on here—he was such a great help. There never was any hope of getting that job after all. (THINKS... FILLS THE POTS WITH WATER FOR THE VEGETABLES) You know, Annie, I had thought that I would be able to put a few shillings each week into a sinking fund and send it to Mamma to help pay off her debts, but that's impossible. I just can't seem to find a way out. It's a real job for St Joseph.

ANNIE: (FIRMLY) Oh, Mary, be realistic! To keep going like this is to ask for a first class miracle! I think you're taking this way of life a little too seriously. It's never been done before. Most of our relatives expected you to enter the Sisters of Mercy in Melbourne if you wanted to become a Religious. Some of them think that you're going a bit mad.

MARY: (WITH QUIET CONVICTION) I realise that they don't see things the way I do, but what I've chosen is a risk that I must take. *I have an earnest longing for the Order of St Joseph and know well how hard it will be to get it established here—but everything God blesses will prosper...* You see, Annie, while I was meditating the other day, I had a sort of dream.

ANNIE: A dream?... Tell me more. (LOOKS CONCERNED AND CURIOUS)

MARY: *The Bishop seemed to be before me, and I was a sheep. The Bishop went to pull me up with his crook, and then he changed his mind, and the crook looked like one of those things they used to dip sheep when they were washing them.* (ANNIE LOOKS PUZZLED) *And I was a sheep being dipped in the same way...* so you see, Annie, there seems to be meaning in all that has led to this venture, though I'm not sure where it is all leading.

ANNIE: Mary, are you sure that you're not just being hoodwinked by some nonsensical fantasy of your own? I can't help being impressed by all you are trying to do for the children, but don't you realise that you're giving others the impression of an arrogant and stubborn woman with all this talk of a new religious Sisterhood? You know as well as I do how much Mamma would dearly love to have you at home, and you're also aware that we are deep in debt.

MARY: It pains me greatly not to be home with Mamma, Annie, but I've promised God something now, and I dare not turn my back on it... (THINKS)... *How do you write to St Joseph?*

ANNIE: (QUIZZICALLY) Write to St Joseph? Oh dear, Mary... Surely you are referring to Father Woods?

MARY: (BEGINNING TO PACK SOME FOOD PARCELS) Come; help me with these hampers for some poor families... Annie, I'm convinced of one thing.

ANNIE: And what's that?

MARY: We just cannot give up the Penola venture, because the future of too many children depends on it. I'm also convinced that God is calling me to give myself completely to Him... What really prompts me to go on is that Religious Education is in grave danger of being cut out altogether, and I believe that we must introduce a curriculum based on the Love of God, at all costs.

ANNIE: (GIVING UP ARGUING) Well, (SIGHS) there's no doubt about it, Mary, you're a born optimist... but I can't say I share your enthusiasm. I'll help you for as long as you need me for the teaching, but don't think for a moment that I'll take on the Religious Life!

MARY: (SMILES) I am indeed grateful to you, dear Annie, that you are ready to stay on with me, even though you don't see things the same way as I do.
(MAGGIE ENTERS. SHE HAS BEEN SLEEPING IN THE NEXT ROOM)

MARY: Hello, Maggie. Did you have a good rest?

MAGGIE: Yes, thanks, Mary. I just overheard what you and Annie were saying about the Religious Life. I think you are influencing Lexie a bit too much on the matter, Mary. Are you fully aware that she is only fifteen, and she's been saying lately how attractive the Religious Life is to her?

MARY: That's how old I was when I began to think seriously about it, Maggie. Let her make her own choice to come or not.

ANNIE: Oh, I think she should go back to Mamma for a few years, Mary... This kind of life is adventurous and new to her now, but it'll wear off, and I don't know that we should let her take the risk.

MARY: Time will tell, Annie. In the meantime, what we can do is pray.
(MARY KEEPS WORKING)

ANNIE: Well, Mary (SMILING) I can't argue with you there.
(PUTS THE KETTLE ON AND STOKES THE FIRE)

MARY: Julia Fitzgerald, Rose Cunningham and Mary Wright seem to be interested in joining. They told me in their letters that they believe it's worthwhile to join forces in educating the young in this colony.

MAGGIE: You hope against hope, Mary... there's no doubt about that!

MARY: If you'll excuse me, it's almost time for the mail coach to arrive.
(HANDS MAGGIE A CUP OF TEA AND LEAVES)

ANNIE: Really, Maggie, I'm worried about Mary. This way of life is just never going to work.

MAGGIE: Well, you must admit that Mary is very determined to give it a go, and knowing her, she won't give up too easily, especially when she's made up her mind.

ANNIE: That kind of determination is all very well, Maggie, but it becomes a little bit embarrassing and confusing, to say the least, when you hear people say, as I did a man the other day, that she ought to be locked up, and if he was her father, that's what he would do!

MAGGIE: Those are strong words, Annie.

ANNIE: Well, she dresses like a Religious, and yet, the other day, you know as well as I do, that she picked up that sick girl in the street and brought her here, cleaned her up and put her in her own bed, while she slept that night on a mattress on the floor. Nobody else would go near that girl.

MAGGIE: I must admit I couldn't believe my eyes. It's so risky—I think she takes too many risks. All this doing good is great, but there is a limit!

ANNIE: Maybe we ought to stop talking about it, Maggie. You'll never get through to Mary, so I suppose the best thing we can do is to pray.

MAGGIE: I guess you're right, Annie. Time will tell.

ANNIE: (THOUGHTFULLY) Whatever did she mean by asking: "*How do you write to St Joseph?*"
(ORCHESTRA PLAYS FIRE IN THE RED LAND THEME IN PART)

ACT 1

SCENE 3: PENOLA, (MAY 1867)

(THE SCENE IS THE COTTAGE OF JEREMY BOURKE, NEAR PENOLA, SOUTH AUSTRALIA. THE ROOM IS POORLY FURNISHED WITH HOME-MADE BUSH FURNISHINGS. SARAH LIES ILL, IN A ROUGH BED. HER DAUGHTER, JANE, IS SITTING AT THE TABLE RATTLING SPOONS AND PLAYING WITH HER RAG DOLL. SARAH ROLLS OVER TO FACE HER. IT IS LATE IN THE AFTERNOON AND THE LIGHT IS DIM.)

(VOICE OVER: MARY MACKILLOP)
In January, 1867, Bishop Sheil visited our little school for Confirmation and, to the astonishment of all, called me "Sister Mary", thus approving and publicly acknowledging the beginning of a new Religious Order. In spite of this, the new way of life was met with suspicion and opposition from some people in the district. The poor needed us, and it was their needs we strove to meet as our numbers grew. One family in such need was the Bourkes.
(JEREMY ENTERS)

JANE: Daddy, Daddy, you're home!

JEREMY: Aha, my little princess (HE LIFTS HER UP) Oh, I can see you've grown up already. (SEES SARAH IN BED AND PUTS JANE DOWN.) Sarah! Oh, don't tell me you're sick. If only I'd known.

JANE: Jeremy, it's been so long! I thought you'd never come!

JEREMY: And how's young Andy, eh? (POKING HIS CHIN... ANDREW SMILES) If I'd only known you were in a bad way, I would have come earlier. Whatever is wrong?

SARAH: I think it's bronchitis.

JEREMY: Did you call a doctor?

SARAH: There's no money and no doctor, I'm afraid. (IN BETWEEN COUGHS) With David's help I've just had to struggle the best way I could... but now you're home, everything is going to be all right.

JEREMY: David, how are yer, me boy? I can see you've become quite a man of the house!

DAVID: Hello, Dad.

(JEREMY SITS DOWN WEARILY AND HOPELESSLY ON THE CHAIR)

JEREMY: Everything's... er... <u>not</u> going to be all right, Sarah.

SARAH: What do you mean? (ANXIOUSLY)

JEREMY: You see, I haven't any money and my searchin' for work in these parts has been a failure.

JANE: (PERCEPTIVELY) Daddy, aren't we going to be rich?

JEREMY: No, my princess. But Daddy will keep tryin' and you'll see.

DAVID: Dad, I've got bad news for you, too.

JEREMY: (APPREHENSIVE) What's that?

DAVID: This is the last food we've got in the house.

JEREMY: What about the sheep? (IN PANIC)

DAVID: We didn't get enough money, Dad, and we had to sell 'em. This is the last of the lambs we kept. We just thought that you'd be back soon with plenty of money in your pockets.

JEREMY: What about the milk and the cheese and the butter... and the eggs?
(MORE ANXIOUSLY, STANDS UP)

DAVID: Dad, you've been away a long time. We didn't have any money for the labour... an everything's sold.

SARAH: (CRYING) Jeremy... that means we're destitute.

JEREMY: Stop cryin', Love, we'll think of somethin'.

(SARAH STARTS ANOTHER COUGHING FIT, AND JEREMY GOES OVER TO THE BED)

JEREMY: (TO DAVID): Bring your mother a drink, boy. (DAVID BRINGS OVER A GLASS OF WATER).

JEREMY: (THINKING OUT ALOUD) We can't sell the property... we'll have nothin'.
(JANE STARTS TO CRY AND JEREMY PICKS HER UP)

ANDREW: (GETTING OFF HIS CHAIR AND GOING TO THE DOOR. NO ONE TAKES ANY NOTICE) Someone's coming... looks like two ladies in a buggy.

SARAH: Who could be out here this late in the day? Do you know them, Andrew?

ANDREW: No, and they're all dressed funny... all in black with funny hats!

SARAH: That must be the teacher from Penola that I've been hearing about... Father Woods' school teacher. She's some sort of nun, I think... and just look at the state of this place! We've got nothing to offer them.
(COUGHS AGAIN)

JEREMY: We just can't invite them in 'ere, Sarah. I don't want any do-gooders interfering with our privacy. What kind of a provider will they think I am? And you're too sick with bronchitis!

DAVID: (TONE OF ANTICLIMAX, CONTRAST)
They're nearly in time for some of this stew. It's nearly cooked. Maybe they can help us.

SARAH: David has a point there, Jeremy. Maybe they can.

ANDREW: (CALLING OUT) Here they come.

SARAH: You'll have to let them in, Jeremy.

JEREMY: Well, if you're lettin' them in, I'm goin' out... (HE'S TOO LATE)

SR MARY: (TO ANDREW) Well, good evening, young man. (MARY AND ROSE STAND AT THE DOOR, AND ANDREW STANDS BACK TO LET THEM ENTER)

SARAH: (SARAH CALLS OUT FROM THE BED) Come in... Er (SHE CAN'T THINK OF A TITLE) Come in.

(SR MARY ENTERS WITH SR ROSE AND TAKES IN THE SITUATION IN A MOMENT)

SR MARY: Good evening. You must be Mr Bourke?

JEREMY: (HUMILIATED) Yes, I am... er, do excuse the state of this place. You see...

SR MARY: (FEELING FOR HIM) Please don't try to explain. I can see that you've just walked in from a long journey.
(JEREMY RELAXES A LITTLE) This is Sr Rose, and I am Sr Mary.

JEREMY: Er, do sit down. I was just leavin' to pack some tools away. (STILL EMBARRASSED) This is my wife, Sarah.

SARAH: (COUGHING) Please excuse Jeremy. He feels very badly about the way he found us on his arrival home from such a long journey. He's been looking for work in Victoria, you see. Do sit down, Sisters.

SR MARY: We're living in troubled times, Mrs Bourke. I hope we haven't embarrassed you all too much by walking in at this hour.
(SR ROSE NOTICES JANE AND SMILES... PICKS UP DOLL)

SARAH: Sister... we're desperate! (COUGHS) We'll have to have some help.

SR MARY: Don't worry, Mrs Bourke. I assure you that we'll certainly do all we can. Sister Rose, would you help Mrs Bourke, while I help get the children tidied up...

(SR ROSE HAS GONE TO HELP MRS BOURKE TO A CHAIR BY THE BED SO THAT SHE CAN MAKE IT UP. IT HAS NOT BEEN DONE PROPERLY FOR DAYS... DIALOGUE ON ACTION)

SARAH: Sister, you'll have to pardon the way the children are... I just haven't been up to it.

SR ROSE: Never mind, Mrs Bourke. Some good food and a little spoiling will soon have you back on your feet. There's such a lot of sickness about. We have some medicines in the buggy.

SARAH: Thank you, Sister, thank you. (TO MARY) I'm afraid these clothes are all they have.

SR MARY: Don't worry, Mrs Bourke. Our buggy's like a hawker's cart. We even have clothes for big and small, young and old. I'll get them.

SARAH: Andrew will get them for you, Sister.

SR MARY: Andrew, eh. (SHE GOES TO HIM AND TAKES HIS HAND. HE HAS BEEN STANDING WATCHING FROM NEAR THE BED) Now, do you think you're strong enough to carry a portmanteau?

ANDREW: Yes.

SR MARY: Well, you'll see our old one in the buggy... a brown one... would you get it for me, please?

SARAH: You didn't meet David or Jane yet. I haven't sent David to school yet, Sister.

DAVID: I could've learnt a lot better if I had gone to school... but with Dad away, and no money and no chance to go... I never went.

SR MARY: You sound as if you really would like to go to school, David... Maybe Sister Rose and I could help.

DAVID: Oh, what's the use...? We can't afford anythin', especially now, as you can see.

SR MARY: We'll soon see about that.

ANDREW: (ENTERING WITH THE PORTMANTEAU AND STRUGGLING) Here's what you wanted, er...

SR MARY: You can call me "Sister Mary". Thank you, Andrew (SR MARY GOES OVER TO THE CASE) Now, see what we have here. (OPENS THE CASE)

ANDREW (NOT WAITING) Oh, boy, look at all those shirts! All ironed and everythin'.

SR MARY: Would you like to try this one on, Andrew? (PAUSES)... Er, Sarah, would you mind if Andrew tried on some of these clothes?

SARAH: (FROM THE BED) Why, Sister Mary... how could I mind? That's so kind of you. I'm only too pleased and surprised (CONTINUES TO COUGH)

ANDREW: (HAS THE SHIRT ON IN SHEER EXCITEMENT) David... Jane... Mummy... Look at me!

JANE: (AFRAID SHE'S MISSING OUT) You look just great, Andrew... (RUNS FROM THE BED TO THE CASE) Oh, look at all those pretty dresses!

SR MARY: This one looks just your size, Jane.

SR ROSE: (MOVING FROM THE BED) Do let me try one on you, Jane.

JANE: Ooh, yes, Sister Rose.

SR MARY: This is for you, David. (MARY PRESENTS THE FOOTBALL TO DAVID)

DAVID: (DROPPING THE SPOON IN THE POT AND LOOKING AROUND FOR THE FIRST TIME)... I never had a football to kick... too busy choppin' wood... You mean I can have that to keep?

SR MARY: It's yours, David... and there are some clothes here for you too... also some nightwear for your dear mother... you might like to choose that later.

SR ROSE: Take a look at the beautiful princess first. Princess Jane! (JANE STRUTS AROUND VAINLY... AND IS MET BY JEREMY RETURNING)

JEREMY: Jane, what's going on here?

JANE: Daddy... Daddy, look at what Sister Mary and Sister Rose gave me.

JEREMY: Gave you? Why, er... Sisters... I have no money to pay for these things... I...

SR MARY: Believe me, Mr Bourke, the children can have this clothing. We are not asking you to pay anything.

JEREMY: But I earn my children's keep... I always have... that is, until bad days struck... but I promise... I'll pay you back.

SR MARY: Seeing the joy in the children's faces is payment enough, Mr Bourke. Please don't feel badly about it. These clothes are not ours either. They've been donated and you're entitled to them.

JEREMY: (RELUCTANTLY, BUT HEART WON BY THE EXCITEMENT OF ANDREW, AND THE JOY ON THE FACE OF JANE, AND THE AMAZEMENT AND HOPE OF SARAH)
Well, Sister Mary, you've brought a little sunshine into the family, in such a short time, I must admit (SITS DOWN AT THE TABLE, FEELING TIRED AND WITHOUT HOPE)
Look, tell me... Where do I go from here? There's no hope of me gettin' a job. I'm really broke, and that's it. There's no way of lookin' after Sarah properly... the kids'll soon be starvin'. What's the use of livin'?

SR MARY: I understand how you must feel this way, Mr Bourke, but I'm sure that if we all work together and take one day at a time, we can work something out.

JEREMY: But you've got all your other work to do... What did you have in mind, Sister Mary?

SR MARY: Well, firstly, Mr Bourke, both Jane and Andrew could come to school and that would take them off Sarah's hands, to give her a chance to recuperate. David would need to stay home for the present.

JEREMY: But I'll never be able to pay the school fees... and anyhow, I've never been too good on religion, you know... It doesn't seem right.

SR MARY: God has provided for us so far, and I don't doubt He will continue to do so. (SMILES) I'll have to enquire further, though, about the possibility of a job for you. Father Woods might help. Would you give me a few days or so?

JEREMY: (A LITTLE HOPE IN HIS VOICE) D'yer really think there's hope of me gettin' a job in these parts? Anywhere?

SR MARY: Well, anyway, it's worth a try, given the right contacts.

SR ROSE: What sort of work do you do, Jeremy?

JEREMY: Mostly labouring work or farm work... never went to school... but I'm good with me hands.

SR ROSE: I'm sure there are many people is these parts who are in need of a labourer... Don't worry, Mr Bourke. Things will work out for the best.

SR MARY: The main thing at the present seems to be to get help for your wife every day. I know some ladies who would come over until Sarah gets well, that is, if you wouldn't mind.

JEREMY: Why are you worrying about my family? I've never yet met anyone who cared as much as this before... Why are you doin' all this? And we don't even go to Church!

SR MARY: You've got a right to live in peace, even in these troubled times; we didn't come here to pass judgement on you, but to be of some small assistance. We believe that you and your family are important.

JEREMY: (THINKING)... It's such a long time since I went to Church. Why would God suddenly care about me... or my family?

SR MARY: Mr Bourke, God really has all the time, but when we're going through the dark patches, it's hard for us to see. I have had the experience in my own family, so I know what you are talking about, and so many people today are nearly desperate... But the worst thing we can do is to stop counting our blessings. *Our greatest crosses and trials are really hidden blessings.*

JEREMY: Well, I don't know how you work that one out, Sister Mary. I never thought anything as good as this would come into my life, earlier this afternoon, when I saw those I love and want to provide for in such a hopeless mess.

SR MARY: You've been blessed with a beautiful wife and family, my dear Mr Bourke, and you've obviously had quite a battle... Sister Rose and I appreciate this, and believe you have done what you could... Don't be too hard on yourself. We'd best be going now, and let you finish your evening together. (GOES OVER TO SARAH)... We'll be back tomorrow, and I'll arrange to have a nurse in. The two youngest can come to school. We'll arrange transport for them in a horse and cart.

SARAH: Sister Mary, and Sister Rose, how can I ever thank you enough?

SR MARY: You deserve it, Sarah... God bless you... Goodbye... Mr Bourke and thank you, David... We'll be visiting you again.

DAVID: Thanks a lot, Sister Mary.

SR ROSE: Goodbye to you all... and Jane, look after your new dress. Goodbye, Andrew.

ANDREW: Goodbye, and come again soon.

JANE: (RUNNING UP TO SISTER MARY AND SISTER ROSE AND KISSING THEM) Goodbye, Sister Rose... and you, too, Sister Mary.
(THE SISTERS EXIT)

SARAH: (TO JEREMY) It looks as if there is some hope at last, dear Jeremy... It's good to have you home.

DAVID: (PEERING INTO THE PORTMANTEAU) Just look at all they gave us!

JANE: An' my new dress!

ANDREW: They're beaut, Dad!

JEREMY: I've never heard of nuns travelling around like they are. These women are different from anyone I've ever met. What are they getting out of it? They made me think... They didn't make a man feel that he was good for nothin', and that's how I felt when I was comin' in here, and seein' you all like this... They didn't just talk... They acted... (TURNS TO SARAH) Me dearest Sarah, it's great to be here.. Sorry I didn't come home with the goods, Love, I tried, really I did.

SARAH: I know, Jeremy. I know... but you're here now and that's the main thing.

DAVID: We all missed you, Dad... I even cut me foot on the axe this mornin'.

JEREMY: Did you, lad? Sorry to hear that. Show me.

DAVID: (UNCOVERING THE BANDAGES) Aw, it'll be all right, Dad. It doesn't hurt any more.

JEREMY: Good on you, Lad.

DAVID: I can't wait to kick me new football, Dad.

ANDREW: I'll be wearin' my new shirt, Dad (GETTING A WORD IN)

JANE: (SWEETLY) An' I'll be wearing my new dress.

JEREMY: (PICKING UP JANE) Come on now, all of you to bed. We've had a big day. Come on, Princess.

(ALL OF THE CHILDREN EXIT... JEREMY GOES BACK TO THE BEDSIDE OF HIS WIFE AND SITS BESIDE HER AS THE CURTAIN CLOSES)

(TRUMPET PLAYS CHORUS OF "FIRE IN THE RED LAND" THEME)

FIRE OF CHRIST'S LOVE

ACT 1

SCENE 4: THE PROFESSION OF MARY MACKILLOP: GROTE STREET, ADELAIDE, SA (15 AUGUST, 1867)

(PRESENT: TWO NOVICES, ROSE CUNNINGHAM AND CLARE WRIGHT AND A POSTULANT, JULIA FITZGERALD—OR FR WOODS AND MARY ONLY.)

ORCHESTRA PLAYS ONE VERSE OF 'ASSUMPTA EST' AS CURTAIN OPENS ON CHAPEL SCENE. (SPOT ON MARY) MARY WALKS TOWARDS THE ALTAR; BEGIN SINGING HYMN AT THE BEGINNING OF THE SECOND TIME PLAYED.

(VOICE OVER: MARY MACKILLOP)
At twenty-five years of age, I made my Religious Profession as a vowed Sister of St Joseph, in the Grote Street Chapel in Adelaide on the 15th of August, 1867. What a joy that day was for me—to give myself to God.

ASSUMPTA EST (Dom Moreno)

Assumpta est Maria
Assumpta est Maria in coelum
Gaudent Angeli (2)
Collaudantes benedicunt Dominum
Alleluia (5)

(MARY KNEELS AND PROSTRATES HERSELF AT THE FOOT OF THE ALTAR FACE DOWN. SHE WEARS A CROWN OF FLOWERS ON HER HEAD, A WHITE VEIL AND A BLACK DRESS... (THE SISTERS WORE BLACK AT THIS STAGE). MARY RISES AND KNEELS BEFORE FATHER WOODS WITH HER HANDS JOINED IN HIS AS A SIGN OF PLEDGING HERSELF TO GOD THROUGH THE CHURCH.)

SR MARY: In the Name of God. Amen. I, Sister Mary of the Cross, being of sound mind, do hereby of my own free will, dedicate myself to the service of God in the Institute of St Joseph, according to the Rules of that Institute and I promise and vow by a simple vow to observe Poverty, Chastity and Obedience, and to promote to the utmost of my power the Love of Jesus, Mary and Joseph in the hearts of little children. And I pray you, Holy Father, and these Sisters who kneel around me, to bear witness in faithfully discharging these obligations, so that I may appear without shame before the judgement seat of Our Lord and Saviour Jesus Christ. I make these vows of my own free will, without coercion or constraint of any kind; and I do so for the pure honour of the Sacred Heart of Jesus, and the Holy Mother of God, St Joseph and St John the Baptist. Under the keeping of our glorious patriarch and patron, I hope to keep them inviolate to the end of my life.

ALL: Amen

FR WOODS: (BLESSING THE RING) Bless this ring, and may the one who wears it remain faithful to you, O Lord. (PLACING THE RING ON MARY'S FINGER) I espouse you, Mary of the Cross, to Jesus Christ, the Son of the Supreme Father, and may he keep you inviolate. Receive, therefore, this ring as a pledge of faith and a seal of the Holy Spirit, that you may henceforth be considered the Spouse of God, and if you are faithful in serving him, by him you shall be eternally crowned.

"FIRE IN THE RED LAND" THEME

(MARY LEAVES THE CHAPEL WHILE THE CHOIR SINGS OR AUDIO IS PLAYED)

Before Federation, Mary shared that vision
God's burning love she longed that all would see
A new congregation fanned the inspiration
Given by the Spirit to set God's people free.

Chorus: Fire in the Red Land,
Kindled by Spirit's Power,
Caught by a loving hand,
Fanned to consuming desire.
Children's praise swells up to you.
Hail to our mother in God.

(SISTER MARY RE-ENTERS, WEARING A CROWN OF THORNS, AND CARRYING A WOODEN CROSS ON HER SHOULDERS. MARY KNEELS.)

SR MARY: I have chosen to be an abject in the House of the Lord, rather than dwell in the tabernacle of sinners. I desire no other crown in this life but a thorny one, and no glory, save in the Name of Christ, and I beg the blessing of the Church on my undertaking.

SALVE JOSEPH

CHOIR: *Salve Joseph, Custos pie,*
Sponse virginis Mariae
Educator optime (Repeat for Chorus)

Per te cuncti liberemur
Omni poena quam meremur
Nostris pro criminibus.

Salvatorem deprecare
Ut nos velit liberare
Nostrae mortis tempore.

(THOSE PRESENT EMBRACE MARY [OR OMIT THIS INSTRUCTION IF THE DIRECTOR DECIDES THAT JULIAN AND MARY ARE ALONE IN THIS SCENE])

(CURTAIN CLOSES) (*See page 54 for translations that may be included in the program.*)

ACT 1

SCENE 5(a): THE EXCOMMUNICATION AND FOLLOWING EVENTS, FRANKLIN STREET, ADELAIDE (21 SEPTEMBER 1871)

(ENCOUNTER WITH FR HORAN)
(VOICE OVER: MARY MACKILLOP)
The joy of my Profession in 1867 was indeed shortlived, as the events of 21st and 22nd of September 1871 unfolded.

(MARY MACKILLOP IN THE PRESENCE OF SR TERESA–FR HORAN HAVING EXAMINED THE SISTERS)

FR HORAN: The Bishop wants you to go to St John's and not to Bagot's Gap as he said at first. You are to go by the first train in the morning.

SR MARY: Father, I particularly wish to see his Lordship first. There are several things about which I wish to speak to him.

FR HORAN: I do not think the Bishop will see you, but I will gladly convey your message.

SR MARY: So much has been said about the Rule being changed that I would like to ascertain what these changes are.

FR HORAN: There will be choir and serving Sisters.

SR MARY: Father, that ruling changes the spirit of the original Rule, which directs that there is to be no distinction among the Sisters.

FR HORAN: I do not agree with you, Sister Mary. Each convent is to be under the control of the local Pastor and will have no connection with the town house. There will be no centre of appeal but the Bishop.

SR MARY: Such an arrangement, Father, would be quite opposed to the Rule. I could not in conscience remain under these changes. I would prefer to take up the alternative the Bishop offered.

FR HORAN: I have read your letter to the Bishop. I strongly disapprove of it.

SR MARY: Father, could we not call a Chapter of the Sisters according to the Rule and lay the Bishop's wishes before them?

FR HORAN: The Bishop is your Chapter. His wishes will be sufficient.

SR MARY: Then could we not delay the matter until Father Woods returns? He has so much to do with the Institute, being its founder.

FR HORAN: (INDIGNANTLY) The Bishop will not listen to Father Woods any more than to anyone else. The Sisters think more of Father Woods than they do of the Bishop, but Father Woods is not the Bishop!

SR MARY: Father, in so far as Father Woods is concerned, it does not matter whether we have him for our Director or not, but it does matter if the Rule is altered.

FR HORAN: Then I suppose you won't go to St John's tomorrow?

SR MARY: Father, how can I under those rules?

FR HORAN: His Lordship will see you in the morning. (EXIT)

ACT 1

SCENE 5(b): FRANKLIN STREET, ADELAIDE CONVENT CHAPEL (22 SEPTEMBER 1871)

(VOICE OVER: MARY MACKILLOP)
Late that evening I left it to the Sisters to make their own decisions as to whether they would accept a new Rule or not. Between ten and eleven o'clock on the night of the 21st September, Fr Horan returned to the Convent saying that, in consequence of my rebellious conduct in not complying with His Lordship's wishes, he had excommunicated me. He gave the message to Sr Teresa. Sr Teresa relayed it to me, as I had retired on account of illness, and she then returned to tell Fr Horan that every Sister held the same opinion about adhering to the original Rule. So it was on the plea that I refused to go to St John's that the following event took place.

THE EXCOMMUNICATION

(THE STAGE IS DIM... THERE ARE A NUMBER OF SISTERS IN THE ORATORY. MARY GENUFLECTS AS IF TO LEAVE, BUT IS INTERRUPTED BY THE FOOTSTEPS OF THE BISHOP IN FULL ECCLESIASTICAL ATTIRE. THE CENTRE OF THE BACK CURTAIN IS LIT UP BY A CROSS. MARY STEPS BACK, TO LET THE BISHOP PASS. THERE IS AN AIR OF APPREHENSION.)

THE BISHOP: Sister Mary, kneel down. (SISTER MARY OBEYS) For your disobedience and rebellion, I have to pronounce on you the awful sentence of excommunication. You are now cut off from membership of the Church, from its Sacraments while living and from Christian Burial when dead. You are now Mary MacKillop free to return to the world, a large portion of the wickedness of which, I fear, you have brought with you into this Institute. The devil of spiritual pride, and a false spirit of religion, has been allowed entrance into the sisters.

(MARY REMAINS PERFECTLY CALM EXTERIORLY, AS IF IN A TRANCE. ONE OF THE OTHER SISTERS SOBS LOUDLY, AND GOES TO KNEEL WITH MARY. THE BISHOP BECKONS MARY TO RISE, WHICH SHE REVERENTLY DOES, AND WALKS STEADILY, AS IF IN A TRANCE, TOWARDS THE DOOR. SOME OF THE OTHER SISTERS RISE TO GO WITH HER, BUT ARE CALLED BACK BY THE BISHOP.)

THE BISHOP: All other Sisters, come back!! There will be no contact with the excommunicated party.

SR MARY'S RESPONSE

(DARKNESS EXCEPT FOR SPOT ON MARY SAYING THE WORDS AS SHE MOVES TO FRONT STAGE)

MARY: *"I really felt like one in a dream. I seemed not to realise the presence of the Bishop and priests. I know I did not see them, but felt, oh, such a love for their office, a love, a sort of reverence for the very sentence which I then knew was being in full force passed on me. I do not know how to describe the feeling, but I was intensely happy, and felt nearer to God than I had ever felt before."*[10]

10. Mary MacKillop to Father Woods, September 1871

(CURTAIN CLOSES)

(VOICE OVER: MARY MACKILLOP)
Six months later, the Bishop, a dying man, admitted that he had been led astray by bad advisors. He bitterly regretted his action against me and the Sisters, and pronounced that I was innocent of the charges laid against me. During that period of time, much to my regret, articles were written in the newspapers condemning the Bishop's action and that of some priests. Father Tappeiner sj, my director, who had given me Holy Communion during the five months of my excommunication, advised me to go to Rome to gain full approval of our Rule.

INTERVAL

Mary MacKillop in her religious habit, 1868

Fr Woods in riding gear, 1866

John MacKillop

Alexander MacKillop (Mary's father)

Flora MacKillop (Mrs MacKillop)
(Mary's mother)

Fr Donald MacKillop sj

Peter MacKillop

Annie MacKillop

Maggie MacKillop

Lexie MacKillop (Alexandrina)

Fr Charles Horan ofm

Bishop Lawrence Sheil ofm

Sr Francis Xavier (Blanche Amsinck)

Sr Josephine McMullen

Sr Francis (Julia Fitzgerald)

Sr Monica Phillips

Sr Calasanctius Howley

Fr Joseph Tappeiner sj

Sr Laurentia Honner

Sr La Merci Mahony

ACT 2

SCENE 1: KENSINGTON CONVENT, ADELAIDE SA (1875)

(A PRELUDE TO THIS SCENE IS THE PLAYING BY THE ORCHESTRA OF "WALK HUMBLY WITH YOUR GOD.")

Refrain:
This is what Yahweh asks of you, only this:
That you act justly, that you love tenderly,
That you walk humbly with your God.

1. *My children I am with you such a little while*
   And where I go now, you cannot come
   A new commandment I give to you
   As I have loved you, so love each other.

2. *Do not let your hearts be troubled*
   Trust in God now, and trust in me
   I go to prepare a place for you
   And I shall come again to take you home.

3. *Peace is the gift I leave with you-*
   A peace the world can never give
   If you keep my Word, my Father will love you.
   And we will come again and make our home.

KENSINGTON CONVENT (1875)
(THE CONDITIONS ARE VERY CROWDED. THERE ARE BEDS MADE UP IN THE LIVING ROOM AND ALONG THE PASSAGEWAY BETWEEN THE ROOMS, ON THE VERANDAH, AND IN THE TENTS IN THE YARD. TWO SISTERS, MONICA AND CALASANCTIUS ARE ATTENDING TO THE LAST PART OF THE TIDYING UP OF BEDS PRIOR TO THE ARRIVAL OF MOTHER MARY, WHO HAD BEEN AWAY IN ROME SEEKING THE APPROVAL OF THE RULE. SISTERS ARE MAKING BEDS FOR THE POSTULANTS ON MATTRESSES ON THE FLOOR.)

(VOICE OVER: MARY MACKILLOP)
In 1875, I returned to Kensington from my long voyage, carrying with me a Constitution, written by a Dominican, Father Bianchi. I brought back with me fifteen young women from Ireland who were interested in becoming Sisters of St Joseph of the Sacred Heart.

(MOTHER MARY ENTERS; SHE HAS WITH HER SOME OF THE FIFTEEN IRISH POSTULANTS. TWO SISTERS IN THE BACKGROUND CONTINUE TO MAKE BEDS.)

SR CALASANCTIUS: Mother Mary! (THEY EMBRACE)

SR MONICA: It's been so long! (ALL ARE WELCOMED)

M.MARY: How wonderful to be back at last! How are you all? I can see that you're really crowded out.

SR CAL.: It's been rather a crush to fit everyone in, but we're struggling along happily, and rather grateful to have such a big family.

M.MARY: Even so, these are really trying conditions for you. We'll have to make some arrangements for outside accommodation.

SR MON: And finding somewhere to fit all the postulants! I'm sure they'll notice a vast difference between this and their own homes in Ireland.

M.MARY: Well, at the moment they seem so excited that they're ready for anything. I did try to prepare them for what they would have to face, so I do hope they can stand up to it.

SR CAL: How are you, Mother Mary?

M.MARY: Tired, my dear Sr Calasanctius, but, oh, so happy to be home at last.

SR MON: I really am quite amazed at the number of postulants you were able bring back with you. They must have been very convinced if they were ready to leave their own country.

M.MARY: I did make an effort to give them the truth about the deprivation we all experience... and I suppose the spirit of adventure was very much alive in them as young people. I explained to them the great need there was in this country for dedicated people, and this fired some of them with enthusiasm to help out.

SR CAL: I'm just thinking about where we can put them all up... there's really no room here.

M.MARY: The first thought that came to my mind was the possibility of the "Solitude" across the road.

SR CAL: Yes, we could find room there at the moment, at least until we can get somewhere else... (CHANGES SUBJECT)... but I'm sure you've lots to tell us about your journey home... did you enjoy it?

M.MARY: Yes, indeed, Sr Calasanctius. (PAUSES REFLECTIVELY) One of the highlights of it was that I was able to enjoy the presence of the Blessed Sacrament for part of the journey.

SR MON: And how did this come about?

M.MARY: Fr Murray brought the Blessed Sacrament to my cabin in the pyx case. I kept the lamp burning before it.

SR MON: That sounds wonderful! Sister Calasanctius and I are looking forward to hearing what you have to say about the Rule, Mother.

M.MARY: I'll have to write and tell all the Sisters about this, Sister Monica. You see, what I took to Rome was merely a working paper, not a Constitution. So Father Bianchi, a learned Dominican priest, did us a great service by formulating a proper constitution for us to follow.

When you read it, you'll see what I mean about the fact that there are a few changes here and there, which will make the Rule more workable and adapted to our circumstances. The Rule as it is now has been given to us on trial before it is finally approved by our Australian Bishops.

SR CAL: From your letters, I gathered that you found great assistance from the authorities in Rome.

SR MARY: Yes, I did, Sr Calasanctius, and I don't think I could ever be grateful enough for the kindness that was shown to me there. *Nothing humbles me more than consideration shown by ecclesiastical superiors.* Monsignor Kirby was really understanding, and was kindness itself. That compensated for much of the loneliness I felt being so far away from you all.

SR CAL: And we missed you so much, too. So what happens now about the Rule?

M.MARY: Well, first of all, we'll have to call a General Chapter so that the Rule might be explained to all the Sisters. Cardinal Franchi from Rome has stipulated that this take place on the 19th of March. I do miss the presence of Father Woods in all this, though. How is he really, Sister Monica?

SR MON: He's over in Tasmania at the moment, and, I'm afraid, still rather upset that you took the advice of others in going to Rome so soon, and particularly that you did not see him beforehand. I don't see that he will be happy about any of his ideas being changed in this new Rule.

M.MARY: The fact that he is in such distress is a great cause of pain for me, Sisters. I, too, was upset that I was unable to see him before going to Rome, in those circumstances, with Father Tappeiner as my director, and Father Woods having been sent away after the storm of the excommunication, but I acted in the way I thought best at the time, and prayed that I would do what God wanted.

SR CAL: Father Woods is still against the idea of the Sisters owning any property, and still wants to hang on to the ideal of Franciscan poverty in its literal sense.

M.MARY: That is what we both wanted in the beginning, but with Sisters dying of consumption and starvation, and with the prospect of their being evicted by a bishop in the way that Bishop Sheil evicted us from Franklin Street, Rome's authorities have instructed us to own some property for our own security. However, one consolation I'm sure Father Woods would be pleased to hear, is that the concept of our being centrally governed, rather than being under diocesan control, was fully endorsed by Rome. Both the Bishop and I will write to him and explain everything.

SR CAL: I can share your distress in the fact that Father Woods misunderstands your position, and all the more, because he was with us in the beginning.

SR MON: Do tell us about your visit to the Holy Father... We've all been looking forward to hearing it from your own lips.
(WHILE MOTHER MARY SPEAKS, SHADOW PLAY OF THE EVENT OCCURS AT THE SIDE)

M.MARY: My dear Sisters, this was a most overwhelming occasion for me. When word somehow leaked out that I was the excommunicated one (SPEAKS SOBERLY), *the Holy Father singled me out and showed me that he had a father's heart.* As I told you in the letter, the Holy Father blessed me, and the Institute, and all our intentions. Monsignor Kirby was most kind, and presented me to the Holy Father and translated to me what the Holy Father had said. Those moments were more dear to me than I will attempt to say, or even hope to express.

SR CAL: Thank you for sharing that with us, Mother Mary.
(ALL MARVEL IN REVERENT SILENCE)

M.MARY: Thank you for the great welcome, Sisters. I really do appreciate it.

SR CAL: It's more than a pleasure, Mother Mary... just to see you again.

SR MON: It's grand to have you home.

M.MARY: *How it must gladden Heaven to see a community in peace.*

(SOLO ON MICROPHONE SINGS)
A Priest of God in the days of the gold rush
Shared Mary's dream of Australia in unity.
His missionary heart on fire with Christ-love
Led him to believe in the power of Community.

CONSUMING FIRE

ACT 2

SCENE 2: HOTEL AT WILMINGTON, SOUTH AUSTRALIA, (1878)

(VOICE OVER: NURSE)
My memories of the courage and fearlessness of Mother Mary MacKillop take me back to the events of 1878 at Port Augusta. Sr Laurentia was helping Sr Immaculata trim the lamp in the church after Benediction. Though a very young Sister of nineteen years, Sr Laurentia had trouble with her sight. She turned the wick too low, and the lamp exploded. Many people gathered, put out the fire and wrapped Sr Laurentia in a rug and carried her out.

Mary MacKillop was in Adelaide on business. That day's boat for Port Augusta had already left and so Mary caught the train to Burra, a town about half way between Adelaide and Port Augusta. This is where the train stopped. Mary then took the daily coach from there to Wilmington, some miles from Port Augusta. Mary called in to the local hotel to get help to finish her journey. As it was too dark and dangerous, one of the locals at the bar took Mary first thing the following morning.
(HOTEL: MARY ENTERS THROUGH THE MEN STANDING THERE, AND GOES TO THE BAR)

M.MARY: Excuse me, gentlemen. (ALL LOOK IN AMAZEMENT) Would anyone here be able to lend me a horse to finish the journey to Port Augusta to visit a dying Sister?

FARMER AT BAR:
(IN ASTONISHMENT) Who is this coming in here at this hour?

M.MARY: I repeat—this is an urgent matter. Would you have a horse I could borrow, Sir?

FARMER: What are you doing here in the dead of night? It's not safe for a woman to travel alone in these parts.

M.MARY: Sir, it's as far as the coach would take me. I must get to Port Augusta. Time is moving on, and every minute is precious. Sir, I beg of you...

FARMER: Well, all right, if it's as urgent as that. I'll take you in my horse and buggy. I've never seen or heard of this before!

M.MARY: You are most kind, Sir. Sister Laurentia is not expected to live.

FARMER: Er... What's your name?... er...

M.MARY: Sister Mary of the Cross MacKillop, Sister of St Joseph.

FARMER: Now where have I heard that name before? Aren't you the one they talk about who started a new Order of nuns in these parts? (DRINKS THE LAST DROP OF HIS GLASS OF BEER)
(M.MARY NODS RESPECTFULLY)
THEY LEAVE, THE FARMER SAYING, AS THEY EXIT.
Well, now... let's be off!!

ACT 2

SCENE 3(a): ROOM AT MOUNT STREET, NORTH SYDNEY NSW

(VOICE OVER: MOTHER MARY)
In the latter part of my life, in the years at Mount Street, North Sydney, I had the great joy of meeting Jane Bourke again, but, as you will see, under very different circumstances. I had a stroke and was, at this time, unable to walk.

(MOTHER MARY IN WHEELCHAIR AT HER DESK)

SR LA MERCI: We are busy this morning!

M.MARY: Yes, indeed, Sister La Merci. I wonder who this could be? (SISTER LA MERCI OPENS THE DOOR... JANE BOURKE, NOW A WOMAN OF FORTY-SIX YEARS, STANDS AT THE DOOR)

M.MARY: Why, come in... I recognise your face.

JANE: I know it's way back, Mother Mary, but I've never forgotten you. You gave me a pretty dress, the first pretty one I ever had, at the age seven in Penola, South Australia.

M.MARY: Why, Jane Bourke! After all these years! Sister La Merci, you remember the stories I told you about the visits we made around Penola?

SR LA MERCI: Why, yes, Mother Mary. You visited many poor families.

M. MARY: Well, Jane had a very sick mother at the time I visited them.

JANE: My mother died some years ago; but I must tell you that dear Papa made his peace with God before his death, too. He was so moved by your visit, and I wanted to tell you that, so I enquired to find out where you were when I came to Sydney. I'm so glad to tell you in person.

M.MARY: That's very kind of you, my dear. And I suppose you now have children of your own, do you?

JANE Yes, indeed. I have three grown-up sons. I married one of the boys who used to go to the Penola School. We've had a very happy marriage. If it wasn't for you, I would never have met Jimmy Jones.

M.MARY: So you married Marjorie's son! I'm so happy to hear after all these years. (MOTHER MARY SIGHS)

JANE: Well, Mother Mary (NOTICING HOW TIRED MOTHER MARY WAS BECOMING) Don't let me tire you out! I must be going. (PICKS UP HER THINGS TO LEAVE)

M.MARY: Oh, please don't leave before you tell me how David and Andrew are.

JANE: David had a riding accident ten years ago and was killed.

M.MARY: Oh, I am sorry to hear that... and Andrew?

JANE: Andrew is married and has grown-up children too: two girls and three boys. They moved to Victoria.

M.MARY: Your David falling off a horse brings back memories to me, Jane, about my own brother, John. He was killed in the same way in New Zealand. He was only twenty-two and had been with us in Penola in the beginning.

JANE: How sad it must have been for you in the beginning, Mother Mary!

M.MARY: Not all sad, Jane. *We had many sad things happen to us, but out of all our heart's troubles, He will bring glory to Himself!* (LOOKS AT CRUCIFIX) We have so many joys for which to thank the Lord, too.

JANE: Joys and sorrows indeed. (MAKES AS IF TO BE LEAVING)

SR LA MERCI: Thank you very much for coming, Jane. (SEES HER OUT)

M.MARY: Do come again, won't you, Jane? I'd love to meet your children. I'll never forget the memory of your happy face in your new dress in Penola.

JANE: Neither will I forget the way I felt that day, Mother Mary. (JANE EXITS)

SR LA MERCI: (HANDING MOTHER MARY HER LETTERS) A lot of water has gone under the bridge since those early days. *What a joy to be taken right back to the beginning, where the dream became a reality!*

M.MARY: Yes, that was a great joy for me today. *It does us good to look back a little and see what the Lord has done for us.* (EMPHASISES) *His will is a dear book which I am never tired of reading.*

ACT 2

SCENE 3(b): MOUNT STREET, NORTH SYDNEY NSW (1909)

(ROOM IN MOUNT STREET CONVENT, NORTH SYDNEY (1909)... MOTHER MARY IS AT THE TYPEWRITER. SHE IS TYPING WITH ONLY HER LEFT HAND. SHE IS SWOLLEN IN THE FACE, ENFEEBLED BY THE STROKE, AND UNABLE TO WALK. SR LA MERCI IS WITH HER.)

M.MARY: Sister La Merci, would you kindly hand me over the bundle of letters on the table. I must answer them.

SR LA MERCI: Certainly, Mother Mary. (THERE IS A KNOCK AT THE DOOR... SR LA MERCI ANSWERS) Why, it's some of the boys from Kincumber to see you, Mother.

M.MARY: What a pleasant surprise! Come in, boys! (YOUNG BOYS AGED BETWEEN TEN AND SIXTEEN YEARS ENTER)

PETER: Hello, Mother Mary.

M. MARY: (SHAKING HIS HAND WARMLY WITH HER LEFT HAND) Why hello, Peter. It only seems yesterday that you were rowing me down the river! (THE OTHER BOYS COME UP ONE BY ONE AND ARE GREETED WARMLY BY MOTHER MARY)

M.MARY: And how's the football going lately?

JOHN: (AGED TEN) The big boys always win, Mother. We can't catch them, and they fall on us and we lose the ball.

M.MARY: Never mind, John. It won't be long before you grow a bit taller and stronger, and you'll be a winner then!

JIM: (AGED ELEVEN) We still feel very sad about Philip's death. We're so happy that you made it before he did die.

M.MARY: So am I. I was sad that no priest could come.

SR LA MERCI: Will you ever forget the electrical storm, and how we walked to the cemetery in it?

M.MARY: It was quite a powerful send-off given to little Philip by the Lord. (LAUGHING) I wouldn't be able to do that distance now, would I, Sister La Merci?

SR LA MERCI: I wouldn't guarantee that anything would be impossible for you if you made up your mind, Mother (SMILES)

LESLIE: (AGED THIRTEEN)We miss your visits to us at the Orphanage, Mother. I used to love the boat rides with you.

M.MARY: Well, what good driver would like to wheel me over to my set of drawers (WINKS AT SR LA MERCI) while I see what I can give each of you?

ALAN: I'd love to, Mother Mary. I've got a billy cart now and can drive it down the hill.

M.MARY: Well, as long as you don't go too fast, Alan, you can have a go. (ALAN STRUGGLES WITH THE WHEELCHAIR WHILE THE OTHER BOYS WATCH SOMEWHAT ANXIOUSLY.)

M.MARY: My word, you're not a bad driver at that, Alan. Now, let's see what we have here (PULLS OUT SOME LOLLIES, SOME NOTEPAPER AND CRAYONS) Here you are, now. Have a bundle each to take back with you.

ALL: Thanks, Mother Mary.

M. MARY: Thanks for coming to see me, Boys. It's always a thrill to see you.

BEN: May I wheel you back, Mother Mary?

M.MARY: Why certainly, Ben. I didn't realise there'd be so much competition. (AMUSED)

SR LA MERCI: If you go out into the kitchen, boys, I'm sure there'll be someone waiting for you there.

BOYS: Thanks, Sister La Merci. Goodbye, Mother Mary.

M.MARY: Boys... before you go... I just want to remind you of one thing. Can you remember what I taught you?

PETER: I... I... I think I can, Mother Mary... *the Sacred Heart loves us... and we should keep on loving Jesus.*

M.MARY: That's right. Very good, Peter; please remember that most of all, won't you, boys?

BOYS: We will, Mother Mary (BOYS EXIT)

SR LA MERCI: Well, Mother Mary, so much for the correspondence you wanted to finish.

M.MARY: I'm not worried, Sister La Merci. I really love seeing those young faces again. They're my boys!

FINALE

(CURTAIN RISES. MARY STANDS IN CENTRE OF STAGE. CAST COME UP EITHER SIDE OF THE HALL AND ONTO STAGE DURING THE SINGING OF A VERSE AND CHORUS OF 'FIRE IN THE RED LAND' THEME.)

Franklin Street, Adelaide, SA 1871

Kensington Convent, Adelaide, SA, about 1876

Kensington Convent SA, 2010

Port Augusta SA
Late 1800s

Boys Orphanage, Kincumber NSW, 1906–1909

Mount Street, North Sydney NSW, 1916

ACKNOWLEDGEMENT

The Archives of the Sisters of St Joseph of the Sacred Heart have supplied the photos of the people and places in this Script. All rights reserved. Used with permission.

Chorus Theme: Rev J.W. O'Neill
Verse Theme: Sr Margaret Therese Cusack RSJ

"Fire in the Red Land" Theme

Piano Overture (or Organ)

Orchestrated by Ken Cox

Used with Permission K.Cox

Flute
Violin
ff tutti.
8va
8va

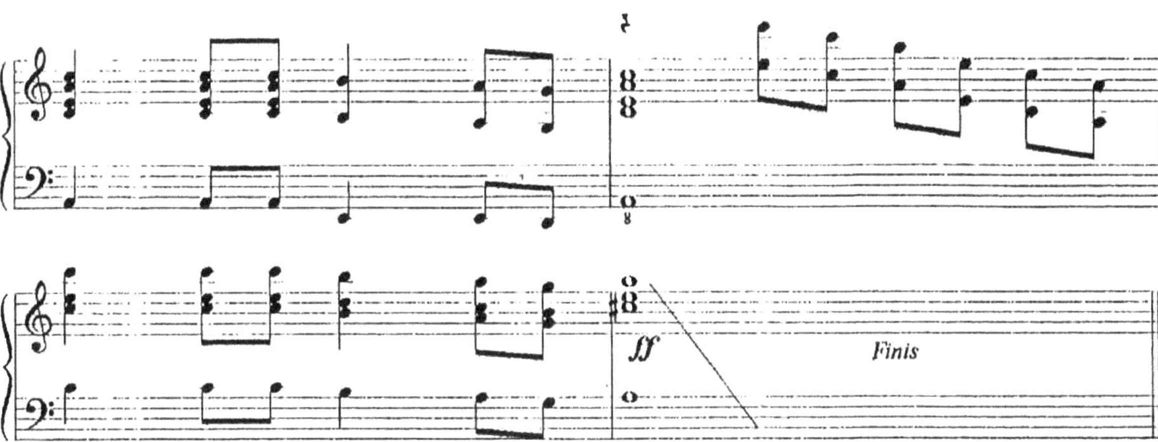
ff
Finis

HYMN
Fire in the Red Land
Chorus by Rev. John O'Neill
(used with permission)
Verse by Sr. Margaret Therese Cusack RSJ
CHORUS
Capo 1
Fmin (Emin) E♭ (D) Fmin (Emin) E♭ (D) Fmin (Gmin) E♭ (D) Fmin (Emin) E♭ (D)
Fire in the Red Land Kind-led by Spir-it's Power Caught by a lo-ving
Fmin (Emin) E♭ (D) Fmin (Gmin) E♭ (D) E♭ (D)
hand Fanned to con-su-ming de-sire Child-ren's praise swells
Fmin (Emin) E♭ (D) Fmin (Emin) E♭ (D) Fmin (Emin)
up to thee Hail to our moth-er in God She was
(Verse)
VERSE
Fmin (Emin) E♭ (D) Fmin (Emin) E♭ (D)
born in the Red Land Nur-tured at God's hand, Ma-ry had a vis-ion of the child-ren's
Fmin (Emin) Fmin (Emin) E♭ (D)
need. There was po-ver-ty and hard-ship sick-ness and suff-ring
Fmin (Emin) A♭ (G) Fmin (Emin) E♭ (D) Fmin (Emin)
lone-li-ness that ma-ny peo-ple would-n't need

14. FIRE IN THE RED LAND
by J W O'Neill and M T Cusack RSJ

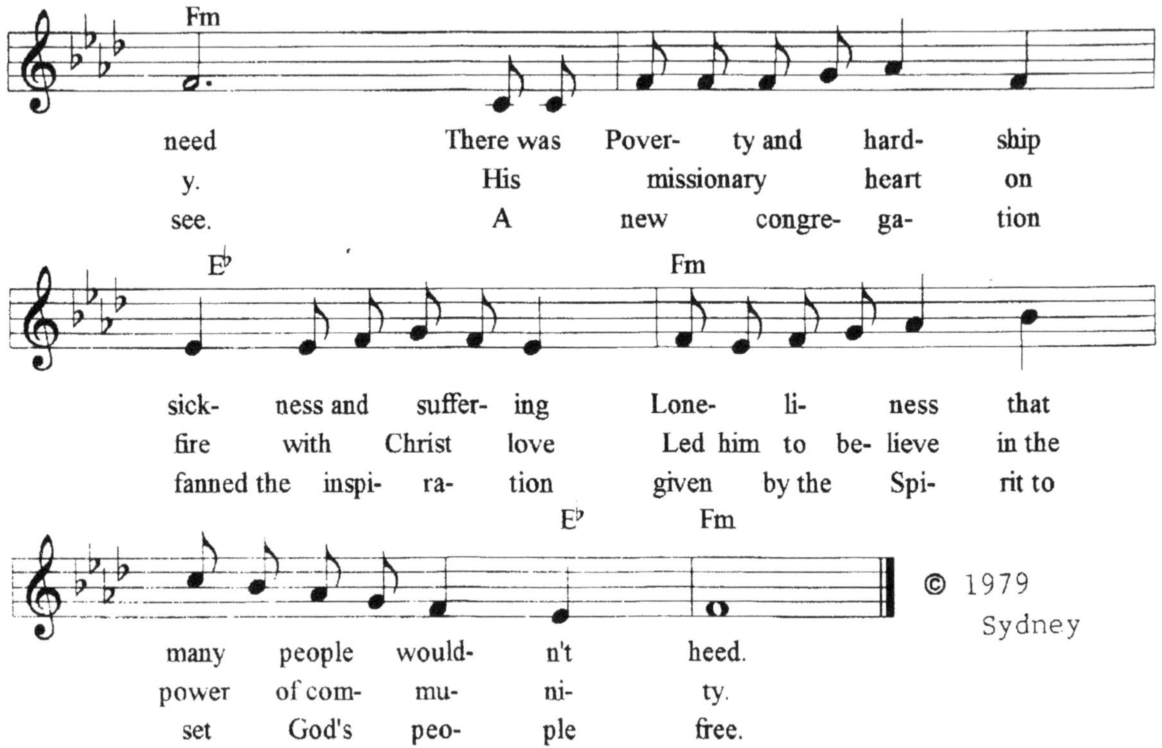

Typeset by Marie Therese Levey rsj

Salve Joseph

Dom Moreno OSB

Assumpta Est Maria

Dom Moreno OSB

gau - dent An - ge - li, col - lau - - dan - tes
Man.
al - le - lu - - - ja,
f
Tutti
f
be - ne - di - cunt Do - mi - num, al - le - lu - -
f
Ped.
al - le - lu - - ja, al - - le - lu - ja, al - - le -
ff
ff
- ja, al - le - lu - ja, al - - le - lu - ja,
ff
- lu - - - - ja, al - le - lu - - - ja.
al - - - lar - - - gan - - do molto
pp
pp
al - le - lu - - ja, al - le - lu - ja.
al - - lar - - - gan - - do molto
pp

WALK HUMBLY WITH YOUR GOD

RECORDED MUSIC
Previously recorded versions of the hymns in this script can be downloaded at https://fireintheredland.bandcamp.com. For further information please contact communications@sosj.org.au.

APPENDIX

CAST
Minimum of 8 adults and 6 children required (children could be student performers).

1. Mary MacKillop
2. Fr Julian Tenison Woods
3. John MacKillop
4. Annie MacKillop
5. Maggie MacKillop
6. Sarah Bourke
   (David Bourke)
   (Andrew Bourke)
   (Jane Bourke)
7. Sr Rose Cunningham
8. Jeremy Bourke
9. Sr La Merci Mahoney
10. Jane Bourke (Adult)
11. Fr Charles Horan
12. Sr Teresa McDonald
13. Bishop Sheil
14. Sr Calasanctius Howley
15. Sr Monica Phillips
16. Nurse (voice over)
17. Farmer(s)
18. Boys from Kincumber
    (Peter)
    (John)
    (Jim)
    (Leslie)
    (Ben)

DOUBLING SUGGESTIONS

ADULTS:

1. Mary MacKillop
2. Fr Julian Tenison Woods/Farmer
3. John/Fr Horan/Farmer
4. Annie/Sister in excommunication Scene
5. Maggie/Sr Teresa/Sr Monica
6. Sr La Merci/Sister in Excommunication Scene/ Nurse (voice over)
7. Bishop Sheil
8. Jane Bourke as adult/Sister in excommunication scene/Sr Calasanctius
9. Jeremy/Farmer

CHILDREN OR YOUTH

1. Andrew Bourke/Peter (orphan)
2. David Bourke/John (orphan)
3. Ben
4. Leslie
5. Jane(small girl)

If children are not available, then, with the exception of Jane, students from theatrical training centres could be used.

(Translations of the following hymns may be included in the program for each production for the benefit of audience understanding.)

Translation of Assumpta Est
Mary, you have been assumed into heaven.
The angels are rejoicing, praising, they bless the Lord.
Alleluia

Translation of Salve Joseph
1. Joseph holy, faithful Guardian, Spouse of the Virgin Mary, best teacher.
2. And from all that we have earned by sin and hearts to evil turned, O free us, Joseph, by your prayer.
3. Then beseech the Saviour for us, That with love he'll come to free us at the moment of our death.

BIBLIOGRAPHY

Oliver, Cathy ed, *Memories of Mary by those who knew her, Sisters of St Joseph, 1925–1926*, (Mulgrave, Vic. JohnGarratt Publishers, 2010)

Sisters of St Joseph, eds, "Thoughts of Our Foundress Mother Mary of the Cross: Sisters of St Joseph of the Sacred Heart." Unpublished document, Archives of the Sisters of St Joseph of the Sacred Heart.

Sisters of St Joseph, eds, *Resource Material from the Archives of the Sisters of St Joseph of the Sacred Heart, No. 4* (Booklet, Sisters of St Joseph, North Sydney, August 1980)

Thorpe, Osmund, *Mary McKillop, The Life of Mother Mary of the Cross* (London Burns & Oates, 1957)

www.ingramcontent.com/pod-product-compliance
Ingram Content Group UK Ltd.
Pitfield, Milton Keynes, MK11 3LW, UK
UKHW050615260726
13967UKWH00009B/2883

9 781925 643404